From the publishers of PASSENGER TRAIN JOURNAL

PASSENGER TRAIN ANNUAL 1987

COMPILED BY PAUL ZACK, MIKE SCHAFER AND KEVIN McKINNEY

COVER: Intercity or commuter, new or nostalgic—passenger trains evoke a special mystique. PASSENGER TRAIN ANNUAL 1987 presents a sampler of the variety found in U.S. and Canadian rail passenger operations. **Main photo:** Amtrak's westbound *California Zephyr* threads the drama of the Colorado Rockies near Debeque on an October 1986 evening ablaze with color (Darrell T. Arndt). **Insets:** Recalling an era past but not forgotten, Southern Pacific's *Shasta Daylight* awaits departure from Oakland, Calif., in November 1960 (Donald R. Kaplan); Maryland Department of Transportation sponsors a modest-but-growing suburban service in the Washington/Baltimore area under the name MARC (Maryland Rail Commuter). At Brunswick, Md., in 1986, the Brunswick Line fleet of rebuilt F-units and secondhand lightweight cars pose for a night portrait (Alex Mayes).

Layout and art production: Mike Schafer/Zephyr Graphics & Editorial, Homewood, Ill.

Color separations, halftones and image assembly: Jim Walter Graphic Arts, Beloit, Wis.

Typesetting: Publishers Studio, Waukesha, Wis.

Printing: Walsworth Publishing Co., Marceline, Mo.

INTERURBAN PRESS
TRANS-ANGLO BOOKS
P.O. Box 6444 • Glendale, CA 91205

1/The Heritage Years

The days of privately operated passenger trains seem so far removed from today's modernized, standardized—and unfortunately skeletonized—Amtrak network. But the *Twentieth Century Limiteds* of New York Central, the *Super Chiefs* of Santa Fe, the *Creoles* of Illinois Central and the *Klamaths* of Southern Pacific will—for better or worse—always remain benchmarks for today's surviving U.S. rail passenger system.

These are the trains of heritage—in terms of route, scheduling, name or even equipment (hence Amtrak's use of the term "Heritage" in denoting rehabilitated cars built for private carriers during the post-World War II era of optimism). Those who are old enough to recall the pre-Amtrak era perhaps cast a different eye on, say, an Amtrak Heritage/Amfleet *Capitol Limited* cruising along the Potomac River behind an F40: A blink of an eye turns the stainless-steel liner into a slip of blue-and-gray (with gold pinstripes) and—wait a minute; is that an F40 or a pair of Royal Blue EA's?

The vision escapes. The only blue we see is that of the Amtrak red/white/blue "cigar band" along stainless-steel cars. And the chant of E-unit engines we thought to hear is drowned out by the whine of the constant-speed engine in the F40. We are content, though, knowing there is a *Capitol Limited* at all in 1987. We wouldn't have guessed as much photographing "The Cap's" last run in April 1971.

And be content, too, that so many photographers captured so much of our passenger train heritage on film. To those whose remembrances of passenger operations of the "good ole days" slip away all too easily without photographic record, and to those not old enough to have experienced green-and-orange Great Northern *Badgers*, red-and-stainless Katy *Texas Specials* or Pennsy's Tuscan red "Blue Ribbon" fleet, we dedicate these Heritage pages!

(Above) Ample head-end traffic and a mixed streamlined and heavy-weight consist denote one of New York Central's lesser-known trains skimming southbound through Garrison, N.Y., in 1949 behind an A-B set of handsome Alco PAs. **(Facing page right)** E7s pause with the westbound *Afternoon Hiawatha* at Milwaukee in 1948. **(Below)** Shrouded in stainless steel, Chesapeake & Ohio 4-6-4 492 contrasts with the heavyweight equipment of the *Sportsman* at Alexandria, Va., in 1948.

Three photos, John Krause

Daniel Gray

E8 No. 2012 of the St. Louis-San Francisco Railway idles at Terminal Station,
Birmingham, Ala., following its overnight trek from Kansas City with the
Sunnyland. Frisco named its E-units after famous racehorses; the 2012 carries
the name *Flying Ebony* under the side cab windows.

Daniel Gray

Prestigious train 1 of the Chesapeake & Ohio, the *George Washington*, departs its namesake city in July 1961 for its overnight journey to western destinations. The train had a number of through-car movements and connecting legs; for example, at Charlottesville, Va., a little over two hours away, No. 1 will combine with its Newport News (Va.)/Richmond section. In the wee hours of the following morning, at Ashland, Ky., the train will split into Cincinnati and Louisville sections, and a Chicago sleeper will be forwarded west of Cincy on New York Central's *James Whitcomb Riley*.

Both photos, Paul Zack

(**Center left**) On a warm spring evening in May 1977, the rush hour is over and things have quieted down at the Joliet, Ill., joint Rock Island/Santa Fe/Illinois Central Gulf station. Presently, a headlight in the east signals the arrival of Rock Island No. 5, the *Quad City Rocket*, stopping to handle one paying patron. Rock's Bicentennial E8 easily works the two-car consist. Roughly a half hour later, Rock Island's other non-Amtrak entry in the timetables noses through Joliet (**left**). No. 11, the *Peoria Rocket*, doesn't even stop tonight—there are no passengers. Rock Island continued these trains until early 1980, longer than expected by most.

5

The *California Zephyr* was still a youngster of nine months when this scene was recorded on Dec. 19, 1949, near Pleasanton, Calif. Power for the sparkling 11-car consist was an A-B-B set of Western Pacific F3s.

Regional carrier Spokane, Portland & Seattle operated the Portland (Ore.) sections of Great Northern's *Empire Builder* and Northern Pacific's *North Coast Limited*. In fact, the rival streamliners were combined into one train on the SP&S, numbered 1 westbound and 2 east. Here, on the afternoon of Aug. 25, 1969, No. 2 is departing Portland behind steam-generator-equipped SP&S F-units. The *North Coast* cars will come off at Pasco, Wash., to join NP's Seattle section, and the *Builder* cars will continue to Spokane, Wash., where they'll meet their GN Seattle section. SP&S, owned by NP and GN, mixed its own equipment into consists between Spokane and Portland, making what was perhaps the most colorful passenger trains in the Pacific Northwest.

Ted Benson

A new schedule for SP's Portland-Oakland *Cascade* found the train leaving Oakland after dark for the first time on March 23, 1969—a change that allowed for an across-the-Bay connection with the Los Angeles-San Francisco *Coast Daylight*, and one that proved a precursor to Amtrak's *Coast Starlight* schedule.

Philip R. Hastings

Northern Pacific RDC2 No. B-32 awaits its departure from Union Station in Winnipeg, Man., as train 14 on Oct. 2, 1969. Destination: Pembina, N. Dak., at the international border. A few weeks earlier, No. 14 would be heading all the way to Staples, Minn., for a connection with the Chicago-Seattle *Mainstreeter*. NP had won permission to discontinue the train—but only in the U.S. Eventually the Canadian segment was dropped as well.

Three photos, Tom Carver

(Above) Pool-train service, Alaska style: Number 1 on the Fairbanks-Anchorage run slips past Nancy Lake in September 1985. (Right) Number 1 again, dwarfed by the grandeur that is Alaska, cruises above cool waters at Matanuska behind A-B F's and an E9A, Aug. 26, 1985. (Below) The odd consist of Alaska Railroad's "Whittier Shuttle" confirms that there's no practical way for road vehicles to get from Anchorage to Whittier other than by rail. The shuttle is at Portage on Sept. 5, 1985.

New York Central 4-8-2 2998 is an imposing locomotive on such a modest train, No. 46, the *Boston Special*, from Chicago, pausing at Dearborn, Mich., in the spring of 1940; additional cars will be picked up at Detroit and Buffalo.

Collection of Lou Marre

(Above) Its streamlined consist broken by a heavyweight RPO and coach, Baltimore & Ohio's *Cincinnatian* of the Cincinnati-Detroit route (the train originally was introduced on the Cincinnati-Washington route) accelerates away from its stop at Lima, Ohio, circa 1955. Tower at right guards PRR's Chicago-Pittsburgh main. **(Right)** Spit-and-polish 4-6-4 No. 1400 of the New Haven readies for its departure from Boston South Station with a lengthy *Colonial* in 1937. **(Facing page, far right)** Jersey Central knew the importance of double-ended locomotives for efficient, frequent passenger schedules. "Camelback" locomotives such as this 2-8-0 on an outbound commuter run at Jersey City Terminal were bidirectional, if somewhat awkward for crews—engineer and fireman were separated by the boiler.

Photographer unknown

Emery J. Gulash

Photographer unknown

Triple E-units march into St. Louis on Aug. 4, 1966, with the *Penn Texas* from New York. The name harked a day when this Pennsylvania run ferried through New York-Texas sleeping cars, but by this time the through cars were a thing of the past.

(Above) When Illinois Central's Chicago-Waterloo (Iowa) *Land O'Corn* was a real streamliner, its path stayed clear for a fast schedule. But by the time this scene was recorded in the summer of 1966, the train had been downgraded to a day local shorn of its streamlined consist, diner-lounge and speedy service. Westbound No. 13 has been put "in the hole" at Buckbee siding, Rockford, Ill., for two noonday eastbound meat trains. IC 4003 leads an E7 and mostly mail consist. (Right) Milwaukee Road's Chicago-Madison service was a popular institution right up to Amtrak. Here E7 18B leads the westbound *Varsity* out of Janesville (Wis.) station and across the Rock River on a warm summer morning in 1965. Train 117 will terminate at the Wisconsin state capital a little after noon and return to Chicago later that evening. Counterpart train on the run was the *Sioux*.

Three Geeps tow Soo Line's *Laker* into Des Plaines, Ill., circa 1960. Despite the town's status as a suburb of Chicago, it will be well over an hour before the train finally arrives at downtown account of its complex entry into the city.

13

Bud Bulgrin

Collection of Lou Marre

Lou Marre

(**Facing page, upper left**) Paired Wabash E8s pause at Mexico, Mo., with train 10-210, the eastbound Domeliner *City of St. Louis*, on Oct. 14, 1961. Wabash provided the Kansas City-St. Louis leg of the Los Angeles/San Francisco-St. Louis operation. Two-story depot in background belongs to Gulf, Mobile & Ohio, whose Bloomington (Ill.)-K.C. route had by this time been freight-only for about a year. (**Above**) Steam-generator-equipped GP9s of the Grand Trunk Western blow through South Bend, Ind., with train 20, the Chicago-Toronto *Maple Leaf*, on Aug. 10, 1965. (**Left**) An FP7 and F3 scream through Haley interlocking at the NYC crossing in Terre Haute, Ind., in September 1963 with Chicago & Eastern Illinois train 92, the Evansville-Chicago day local.

T. O. Repp

(facing page) Queen of Rio Grande rails between Denver and Salt Lake City in the decade of the 1970s was the *Rio Grande Zephyr*, here rolling west through Lynn interlocking Castle Gate, Utah, July 22, 1974. Her immediate predecessor, of course, was the famed CB&Q-D&RGW-WP *California Zephyr* (below) wheeling eastward in the high country near Green River, Utah, on Oct. 8, 1953. An A-B set of Rio Grande PAs and an F3 provided power. (Right) Rio Grande's *Scenic Limited* took the roundabout route between Denver and Ogden, Utah, via Pueblo, Colo., and the Royal Gorge of the Arkansas River (companion train *Exposition Flyer* took the much-shorter Moffat Tunnel Route). In this view looking into the famous chasm circa 1941, we see a 12-car *Scenic Limited* approaching the neck of the canyon, where it will stop for 10 minutes along the Arkansas for patrons to alight and be awed by the abyss. The *Scenic Limited* carried through cars from Kansas City via MP, and passengers wishing to continue to California could simply transfer to the *Exposition Flyer*, which caught up to the *Scenic Limited* at Salt Lake City despite leaving Denver some six hours later.

Dave Salter

Robert G. Stauss, collection of Bill Stauss

Frisco, collection of Louis A. Marre

Frisco Baldwin switcher 207 working the St. Louis yards yields the stage to a bright star from the south, the joint Frisco-Katy *Texas Special*. The publicity photo showed the famous flyer in her new late-1940s garb of stainless steel, with new E7 power.

Collection of Louis A. Marre

One of the less-remarked of those roads owning Alco's famous flat-nosed PA passenger diesels was St. Louis-Southwestern—the Cotton Belt. PA1 301 is at Pine Bluff, Ark., in 1951 with the *Morning Star*, a three-car St. Louis-Dallas local that includes a semi-streamlined Pullman-Standard ''American Flyer'' coach.

(Right) The end of steam is near for Erie, a road built on coal, as the westbound *Erie Limited* makes its station stop at Binghamton, N.Y., in the summer of 1948. The Jersey City-Chicago flagship inherited the *Phoebe Snow* name from Delaware, Lackawanna & Western following merger with that anthracite road in 1960. (Below) Jersey Central owned five double-ended "baby-face" Baldwin DR6-4-20 passenger locomotives, Nos. 2000-2005. The class unit of the series is working westward at Fanwood, N.J., with a local out of Jersey City in 1949. Double-end passenger diesels might not be a bad idea for some of today's passenger operations.

Both photos, John Krause

(Right) Sleek Santa Fe Electro-Motive E1 No. 6 holds at Galesburg, Ill., in April 1951 with what may be the westbound *Kansas Cityan*. **(Below)** Santa Fe gas-electric motor car M186 calls at Joliet (Ill.) Union Station in July 1953. Destination: Pekin (near Peoria), on Santa Fe's only branch in Illinois. Locals called the puddlejumper the "Pekin Chief."

(Above) California classic: The *San Diegan* at its namesake station, May 1970. **(Right)** Bright moonlight adds to the mystique of the evening flight of the all-coach *El Capitan* through the desert east of the San Bernardino mountains in the pre-Hi-Level years.

Santa Fe

Triple General Electric U28CGs sweep through the Arbuckle Mountains of Oklahoma with the *Texas Chief*. Business appeared to be good on the Chicago-Kansas City-Texas run this day.

For at least three generations the overnight Sioux City-Chicago *Hawkeye* of Illinois Central's Iowa Division pulled up just short of Park Avenue in downtown Waterloo a little after midnight. On this April evening in 1967, two E7's provide power for train 12, laden with Flexi-Van, baggage cars, RPO and (out of view) coaches and sleeper.

Eventually IC vacated the depot along the Cedar River in favor of a newer facility on the freight belt around Waterloo. The *Hawkeye*, which once also had Sioux Falls and Omaha sections, succumbed to Amtrak on May 1, 1971.

Philip R. Hastings

Louis A. Marre

The belle of the Kansas City Southern passenger fleet was, of course, the *Southern Belle*, here coasting through Baron, Okla., in November 1962. The Kansas City-New Orleans train was perhaps best known for its splendid black/yellow/red paint scheme.

(Above) The Hotel Dacotah was just a few steps away from the Northern Pacific depot for the traveler arriving from Bismarck, Billings or Butte with business in Fargo, N. Dak. NP train 2, the Chicago-bound *Mainstreeter*, is at the eastern North Dakota city in October 1969. **(Right)** Classy counterpart to the *Mainstreeter* was NP's Chicago-Seattle/Portland *North Coast Limited*. Unfortunately, its sleeper-lounge-observations were bumped from service in the mid-1960s. **(Below)** The westbound *North Coast* drifts into Billings, Mont., in 1969.

David Salter

(Above) St. Louis Car Company and Electro-Motive Corporation teamed up to produce two streamlined motor (or power) cars for Seaboard Air Line in 1936. Nos. 2027 and 2028 protected local and connecting runs in Florida for many years, such as in this scene of power car 2028 wheeling the Tampa-Venice section of the *Silver Meteor*, with a Budd sleeper and coach, south of Durant, Fla., in February 1961. Amazingly, one of the oddball units (the 2028, later 4900) remained in passenger service up until Amtrak, working the Lakeland-Naples (Fla.) section of Seaboard Coast Line's *Champion*. (Right) Central of Georgia's new Budd-built (except for the RPO) *Man O'War* streamliner hastens toward Columbus, Ga., on April 10, 1948. Atlanta was home base for the day turn, which connected at Columbus with IC-CofG Florida runs. (Below) A deadheading heavyweight sleeper breaks the streamlined consist of the joint Pennsylvania-Louisville & Nashville-Atlantic Coast Line-Florida East Coast *South Wind* departing Birmingham, Ala., in August 1946.

David Salter

(Above) Nickel Plate train 5, the *City of Chicago*, slips into its namesake city on a June 1965 morning in the charge of steam-generator-equipped Alco RS11 No. 874. Train 5 and counterpart 6, which had the name *City of Cleveland*, provided an exotic (for fans, anyway) alternate route between Chicago and metro New York; trains 5 and 6 originated and terminated at Buffalo, N.Y., where connection was made with Erie Lackawanna trains to and from Hoboken. **(Below)** Pennsy's finest bangs the diamonds at 21st Street interlocking at Chicago in October 1963. Today's *Broadway Limited* still exits the city through this impressive gateway called the South Branch lift bridge.

25

2/The Amtrak Era

Wayne D. Hills

The variety that existed before Amtrak was maintained in Amtrak's early years as the new rail passenger corporation shuffled cars about in an attempt to maintain an operable fleet. In fact, the variety quickly became a carnival of color as hodge-podge consists showed up everywhere.

The advocates of better passenger service couldn't wait for the day when Amtrak would be able to present an attractive, uniform image to the public. Now, sixteen years and many Amfleet and Superliner cars and F40's later, Amtrak presents its uniform look almost without fail and, many would add, to the point of boredom.

There can be no doubt that without Amtrak, or a creation similar to Amtrak, there would have been no passenger service past 1972 or 1973. Even the highly touted Northeast Corridor was suffering severe prob-

lems of deferred maintenance and declining ridership at that time, and only a special subsidy to Penn Central or a Northeast Corridor authority of some sort would have retained service in the Washington-New York side of the corridor. We can take nothing for granted.

So the fact that we have Amtrak in all regions of the country, usually daily or better, and that ridership, passenger-miles and revenue are generally rising, with or without the help of the oil producers in the Middle East, is nothing short of a miracle, considering the bleak days of the late 1960's and early 1970's.

The down side is that Amtrak is not all it could have been and has yet to reach its full potential. Amtrak was the great leveler: It cleared away the tired equipment and the bare-bones, coach-only, we'll-get-there-when-we-get-there trains, but it also took away much

(Left) The first locomotives purchased new by Amtrak were SDP40Fs, replacing old E and F units formerly owned by private railroads. For the first time, a common face emerged on Amtrak trains across the country. Here, SDP40F No. 570 gets its nose washed at Oakland as it leads the southbound *Coast Starlight* in 1976. **(Below)** Of increasing importance to Amtrak over the years is the Northeast Corridor, the high-speed link between several major Eastern cities. An afternoon *Metroliner* rockets northward under a roof of wires near Monmouth Junction, N.J.

ll is quiet in the very early morning at Ogden, Utah, as Amtrak No. 26, the *Pioneer*, waits or a late *San Francisco Zephyr* from Oakland. Upon No. 6's arrival the two trains will be combined with No. 36, the *Desert Wind* from L.A., and the entire onsist will depart for Cheyanne, Denver and points east. he date is May 23, 1979. Today he *Zephyr/Wind/Pioneer* conerence takes place at Salt Lake ity.

f what was deluxe in the dining experience and large-y rendered first class to the status of token appendage. The bad was gone, thanks to Amtrak, but so was he great.

Thanks to a federally funded rebuild of the Boston-New York-Washington line and state-supported improvements between Los Angeles and San Diego and New York and Albany, Amtrak can point to success tories in the Northeast, Southwest and Empire corridors. Elsewhere the story is different. With the exception of a few state-supported runs, Amtrak seems to have forgotten the Midwest. For example, it has allowed the Chicago-Milwaukee corridor to wither from 14 daily trips in 1971-72 (and nearly 90 in 1963) to as few as six or eight today.

Given the constraints of being a federal corporation and the dubious distinction of being a budget target of four successive administrations—Republican and Democrat—even though all forms of transportation in the U.S. are subsidized, Amtrak has to be given credit for somehow managing to exist and at the same time become the sixth largest American passenger carrier and a billion-dollar company.

But our celebration of "Amtrak at 16" has to be tempered by our knowledge that many important cities and some entire states remain without service, while many others have but one train a day or as few as three a week. Airline travel is increasing at a faster rate than rail travel and it is no wonder when one considers that Amtrak provides only tri-weekly service to much of the fast-growing Sunbelt, including Houston and Phoenix, two of the nation's largest cities.

Mike Schafer

Tom Nelligar

Amtrak sampled a variety of both domestic and foreign-made "train sets" over time, four of which are seen on these two pages. **(Above)** Nameless train 304, one of several Chicago-St. Louis Turboliner runs, blasts through the tiny farming community of Shipman, Ill., on its northbound trek. The four-car turbo set was built in France. **(Right)** Bombardier of Canada supplied Amtrak with two of their LRC sets, one of which poses at South Station in Boston during October of 1980. Operating as Amtrak locomotive No. 38, the LRC was holding down the assignment of train No. 153, the Boston-New Haven *Beacon Hill*.

The sun worshippers at Rocky Neck State Park hardly notice the passage of Amtrak train 153, the daily southbound *Yankee Clipper*, as it glides along the Connecticut coast toward New York City. It's only August of 1975—Amtrak is barely four years old—but the older TurboTrain is showing its wear. This set and Amtrak's one other United Aircraft-built Turbo were retired only a month later.

Ron Johnson

Following the Hudson River route of its predecessor-in-name, Amtrak's *Empire State Express* emerges from Cold Spring tunnel during July 1978. Aesthetically, these American-built (under license) Rohr Turboliners were probably the most attractive trainsets run by Amtrak. They are still in use today.

Tom Nelligan

Joe Blackwell

(Above) One of several *San Diegans*, Amtrak No. 573, cruises north along the Pacific at Del Mar, Calif., some 23 miles out of San Diego on Santa Fe rails. The lone beachcomber's solitude is momentarily broken by the passage of F40 221 and five Amfleet cars. **(Right)** The fireman on the southbound *Coast Starlight* grabs train orders at San Jose, Calif., on Oct. 17, 1981.

Ken Rattenne

(Above) When the westbound *Empire Builder* stopped at Havre, Mont., on Oct. 21, 1983, the lead F40 was adorned with blue protection flags as the train was serviced. **(Right)** One of the trains that didn't last: Four F units lead four domes and other inherited cars as the westbound *North Coast Hiawatha* descends Bozeman Pass near Bozeman, Mont., during August 1973. The *NCH* was dropped from Amtrak timetables in 1979. **(Below)** Train No. 11, Amtrak's southbound *Coast Starlight*, is led by a mixed bag of power (including an ex-Southern FP7) on a dreary March 12, 1977. At Reservation Junction, just north of Tacoma, Wash., No. 11 is only an hour or so into its trip down the Pacific coast.

One of the major attractions along the route of Amtrak trains 7 and 8, the *Empire Builder*, is the spectacular Glacier National Park in Montana. Here, No. 7 pauses at the East Glacier station (the park and its snow-capped mountains lie to the left of this view, out of the picture) on Aug. 26, 1975. Ahead of No. 7 is the climb over Marias Pass on Burlington Northern (ex-GN) rails at the southern edge of the park.

(Below) An early but not permanent name in the Amtrak timetable was the *Coast Daylight*. After several schedule and frequency changes—at this date, November 1972, the train was daily south of Oakland (to L.A.) and tri-weekly north (to Seattle) where it was called the *Coast Starlight*—the name was dropped altogether in 1974. Here, a pleasing array of ex-Southern Pacific FP7's still in railroad colors handles the *Coast Daylight* near San Luis Obispo, Calif.

Karl Zimmermann

T.O. Repp

One of the most breathtaking rail rides in the U.S. is Rio Grande's westward climb up the Front Range of the Rockies out of Denver. Here we share the view of those in the Superliner lounge of the *California Zephyr* as it works its way to the Moffat Tunnel underneath the Continental Divide. Boulder, Colo., is in the distance, and beyond that, miles of high plains.

In any given year, Amtrak runs dozens of special trains for numerous events. On Jan. 8, 1979, a special run of Santa Fe Hi-Levels behind a lone SDP40F waits at a frozen Kansas City Union Station.

Tom Nellig

(Above) Even in the fading light of a cold November day, the outline of a GG1 is unmistakeable. A maze of catenary watches over the "G" and its 18-car Washington-Boston corridor train at Monmouth Junction, N.J., in 1971. A Penn Central business car is behind the locomotive. (Right) Amtrak No. 12, the *Fast Mail*, races through Rowayton, Conn., early in the morning of June 28, 1985. A single AEM7 is enough power for the abbreviated but interesting consist.

Scott Hartley

In the 1980's, the F40 became the mainstay of Amtrak's motive power fleet. Many consider F40s lacking in aesthetics, if for no other reason than their sheer number and omnipresence. But no one can deny the stark and powerful image presented by F40 No. 203, impatiently waiting for the engineer to climb aboard at Boston's South Station in 1984.

In April 1981, the ex-New Haven electrified segment on the Northeast Corridor was experiencing generating station problems. For several weeks, diesel locomotives were used to assist trains from New Haven to the outskirts of New York City. One such rescue mission featured the unlikely combination of an Amtrak RS3 and E8 lending horsepower to an E60 on No. 177, the *Yankee Clipper*, at Milford, Conn.

Paul Zack

(Above) On several occasions during the summer of 1982, Amtrak was forced to re-route trains 5 and 6, the *San Francisco Zephyr*, onto the Chicago & North Western between Chicago and Omaha. Flooding along the regular Burlington Northern route in Iowa necessitated the moves. In July 1982, one of the eastbound *Zephyrs* cruises through the Illinois countryside near La Fox. Because of cab-signal requirements, a C&NW GP50 leads. **(Right)** The northbound *Coast Starlight* of June 1, 1986, stretches across the valley beneath the distant form of Mt. Shasta. Number 14 is making 79 mph here, between Dunsmuir, Calif., and Klamath Falls, Ore. **(Far right)** A Superliner-equipped *Illinois Zephyr* rolls west toward its West Quincy, Mo., terminus on Burlington Northern trackage near Somonauk, Ill. The *IZ*, Nos. 346 and 347, were early haunts for the then-new (June 1982) Superliner lounge cars.

(Above) The northbound Houston-Chicago *Lone Star* rolls away from the station stop at Streator, Ill in May 1979. The *Lone Star* became another of the Carter Administration train-off casualties of late that year. **(Left)** Supplies are fed to Amtrak No. 5 at Chicago. **(Below)** A post-merger combination of Amtrak F units leads the *Empire Builder* out of Chicago Union Station on Milwaukee Road rails i May 1972.

Randy Olson

(**Above**) Among a handful of state-assisted 403(b) trains operated by Amtrak was the Chicago-Dubuque (Iowa) *Black Hawk*. For awhile, Nos. 370 and 371 (372 eastbound on Sundays and holidays) were covered with a set of RDC's. Here, the eastbound *Black Hawk* visits downtown Irene, Ill., in 1975. (**Below**) At Rockford, Ill., in January 1977, a figure on the cold station platform scans eastbound 370, now equipped with a P30CH and Amfleet cars. The *Black Hawk* was discontinued in 1981.

Laird Barber

(Above) Evening at Peachtree Station in Atlanta, Ga., finds Amtrak No. 20, the *Crescent*, pausing for 20 minutes on its northbound run. Until February 1979, this train was one of the "holdouts," operating from New Orleans to Washington, D.C., by the Southern Railway as the *Southern Crescent* (SR Nos. 1 and 2). This view dates from April 1985. (Right) An early experiment by Amtrak was single-train service from Milwaukee to St. Louis, *through* Chicago. The *Prairie State* and *Abraham Lincoln* both had such a routing, and together with a Milwaukee-Detroit run were the only trains to ever operate through Chicago Union Station as a revenue consist. Here, the southbound *Prairie State*, dome-equipped train 301, noses into the Bloomington, Ill., station in April 1973. The through service was ended in October of that same year—cut to Chicago-St. Louis—with the arrival of new Turboliners from France.

After being restored to an original Pennsylvania pin-striped paint scheme, GG1 4877 became a prime attraction on Amtrak's Northeast Corridor. The timeless GG1 styling contrasts with mass-produced Metroliners at New York's Sunnyside coach yard on June 1, 1983.

(Below) Although Amtrak's ubiquitous Amfleet cars don't have the visual appeal of postwar streamlined varnish, their fluted sides are a reminder of that preferred styling of the past. The last light of an October 1984 day glints off the westbound *Illinois Zephyr* as it rolls into the sunset at Eola, Ill.

Bill Meyers

Paul Zack

Don Kaplan

Autumn leaves dot the ballast as Amtrak 303, the daily westbound *Ann Rutledge,* curves into Kirkwood, Mo., on Oct. 23, 1985. About ten miles out of St. Louis, 303 has five hours remaining on its Chicago-Kansas City run.

Alex Mayes

Even a plain F40 and Amfleet cars can create a classic scene of street running. In this case, the southbound *Palmetto* divides Ashland, Va., on Jan. 10, 1982. The New York-Savannah (Ga.) *Palmetto,* Nos. 89 and 90, was a relative latecomer to Amtrak timetables, beginning service in 1976.

(Right and middle right) At milepost 144 on the old Baltimore & Ohio main east of Cumberland, Md., a six-car Amtrak 440 exits Stuart Tunnel and curves through an Appalachian winter. The eastbound *Capitol Limited* will arrive at the nation's capital in about three hours on this March 6, 1982. (Below) In the dead of night at Canton, Ohio, Amtrak's *Broadway Limited* makes its brief station stop. At this date, May 16, 1979, there was no *Capitol Limited*, only a Washington section of the Chicago-New York *Broadway* which was separated at Harrisburg, Pa., and ran to D.C. from there.

Alex Mayes

Alex Mayes

John B. Corns

3/Rush Hour

Ted Benson

(Left) Commuters from arriving Southern Pacific Peninsula commute trains flood SP's old San Francisco terminal at Third and Townsend in July 1973. (Below) Brand-new Chicago RTA (Regional Transportation Authority) F40PHs 100 and 101 pose at Joliet Union Station during dedication ceremonies on Oct. 1, 1977. Trailing the two blue, vermillion and brown units are five former Chicago & North Western bilevel intercity cars owned by Amtrak and leased to the RTA for service on Rock Island suburban routes. Such variety was an example of the increasing complexity of U.S. commuter and transit operations starting in the 1970s with the shift from private operation to new agencies!

In most parts of the U.S. and Canada, commuting means getting into a car or waiting for a bus. But in a few lucky cities, commuting can mean another alternative, the train. Commuter rail is the lifeblood of cities like New York and Chicago. Without it, the center cities would grind to a halt. In Boston, Philadelphia, Baltimore-Washington, San Francisco, Pittsburgh, Toronto and Montreal, commuter rail is an essential element of the people-moving picture.

Rail transit, in the form of rapid (or heavy) rail and light rail, is growing in popularity. The streetcar, all but dead by the 1960's, is making a big comeback as a "light rail vehicle," featuring sleek European designs and offering environmentally sound solutions to congested highways. If only we had been so enlightened in the 1950's, when the abandonment of streetcar lines in favor of buses was considered "progress."

We still have a long way to go. After years of increased transit funding (still small by highway standards), recent years have seen cutbacks in federal funds. Some commuter rail and transit lines have been lost and some continue to struggle. Nevertheless, it is encouraging that virtually every major city in the U.S. and Canada is building, considering building or is already enjoying some form of rail-based transit.

Joe McMillan

Bill Anderson

At the big city end of Rock Island's suburban operations, at La Salle Street Station, stainless-steel and smooth-sided Rock Island bilevel trains stand ready for the evening commuter rush.

Tom Nelligan

SEPTA (Southeastern Pennsylvania Transportation Authority) Silverliner IVs lay over at Trenton, N.J., before returning to Philadelphia on a May day in 1978. Trenton line suburban service out of Philadelphia operates via the former Pennsylvania main line to New York.

Philip R. Hastings

A good share of Pennsylvania-Reading Seashore Line's fleet of Budd RDC1s arrives Camden, N.J. (across the Delaware River from Philadelphia) with a morning commuter run. The impressive train actually started out as a number of trains off various PRSL branches, consolidating at junction points as they moved west. Pennsylvania B-6-class 0-6-0 No. 4035 waits to switch.

Ex-Delaware, Lackawanna &
Western m.u.'s have just left the
Far Hills, N.J., station and are
headed for a station stop at Pea-
pack on the scenic Gladstone
(N.J.) branch in August 1981.

Hal Reiser

John R. Taibi

En route to the teeming shores of the Hudson
River, Erie Lackawanna E8 No. 822 hustles Port
Jervis (N.Y.)-Hoboken (N.J.) commuter train
334 through the pleasant southern New York
countryside between Chester and Monroe in
May 1972. The two-tone green Stilwell coaches
are hand-me-downs from the old Erie.

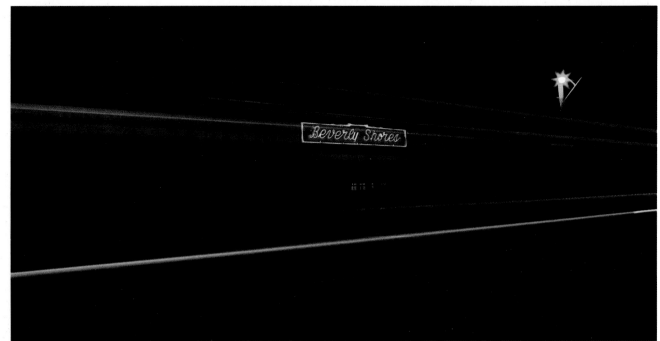

Bruce Stahl

(Above) For years the neon station sign atop South Shore Line's classic Beverly Shores depot (of Insull-era Spanish design) was inoperative. But shortly after new management acquired "America's last interurban" in the middle 1980s, the sign was restored to operation and once again glowed in its evening vigil at the gateway to the little duneland stop in northern Indiana. **(Below)** Not far from Beverly Shores, and in the sun of a pleasant June day in 1982, eastbound South Shore train 4228 skims through the dune country near Portage.

Harvey Kahler

(Above) The throat of Chicago & North Western's terminal in Chicago provides some of the most intense commuter activity anywhere in the Windy City. At Canal Street tower (behind center bilevel), C&NW's North/Northwest Line diverges from the West Line, and commuter trains of all three routes (the North and Northwest lines split farther out at Clybourn) funnel through the elevated junction. In this July 1979 scene, an E pushes its equipment (right train) toward the station as an outbound heads northward. **(Left)** A Milwaukee Road West Line run lays over at Spaulding, Ill., in May 1986. West Line equipment lays overnight at both Elgin and nearby Spaulding. **(Below)** It's a holiday—New Year's Day 1979—so Burlington Northern commuter operations are at a minimum, with most equipment laying over at Aurora during the year's first blizzard. The green E-unit fleet was still going strong in 1987.

Joe McMillan

(Left) Before the new look of SP Peninsula commute service arrived (which by 1987 meant a new San Francisco station, stainless bilevels and silver F40s), Peninsula commute operations meant a Spanish mission-style terminal at Third and Townsend in San Franciso, a mixture of "Roaring Twenties" Harriman-style coaches and smooth-side Pullman-Standard bilevels, and SP hood locomotives—all as depicted in this 1975 scene. SDP45 3201 is departing with train 126 to San Jose. (Below) Account of a backlog of SP commute locomotives undergoing rebuild, SP borrowed Amtrak GE P30CHs to fill in for absent SP units. P30 718 is arriving San Jose on June 1, 1979—the last day these locomotives worked for SP. The big GEs were nearly as high as the bilevels. (Facing page, top) The Harriman cars, SP locomotives and older bilevels are gone now; in their place are sparkling F40s and bilevels operated by Caltrans (California Department of Transportation) for San Jose-San Francisco "Caltrain" service. Train 40 is at Athearn in June 1985.

Harre Demoro

Ken Rattenne

Donald R. Kaplan

Waldemar Sievers photo, collection of Harre Demoro

Today's high-tech rapid-rail system serving the San Francisco Bay Area, BART (for Bay Area Rapid Transit), was predated by the well-remembered—and often missed—Key System interurban. Until Key System gained direct access to downtown San Francisco via the San Francisco-Oakland Bay Bridge (background) in 1939, trains terminated at the Key Ferry Pier partway out in the bay and passengers transferred to ferries destined to downtown. This scene was recorded in 1938, two years after the big bridge, which now serves as Interstate 80, opened to autos. The precursor Key pier opened in 1903 and burned in 1933.

(Above) New Jersey Transit ex-Erie Lackawanna m.u.'s swing through the curve at Milburn, N.J., during evening rush hour in 1984. **(Below)** Two-car North Shore Line train halts at Elm Street station, Winnetka, Ill., on the road's Shore Line route. Silverliner cars such as the 760 (a standard car trails) in this scene were a rarity in revenue service on this line (except when being deadheaded to Highwood shops from their usual haunt on the Valley Line). The Shore Line was abandoned in mid-1955 shortly after this scene was captured.

Lawrence Mack

Owl-eyed Long Beach car 1510 of the Pacific Electric awaits departure time from PE's Los Angeles station at 6th and Main in December 1960.

Donald R. Kaplan

Tom Nelligan

(Above) A Montreal-Vaudreuil push-pull local hurries into Dorval station to rescue waiting passengers from an August thunderstorm in 1982. Commuter runs in Montreal are sometimes referred to as "Town Trains." (Right) GO-GO girls 705 and 707 trail two sets of push-pull rush-hour consists moving from GO Transit's Willowbrook servicing facilities to Toronto Union Station trainsheds (far background) in July 1982.

Brian Nickle

Both photos, Tom Nelligan

(Above) Alco PAs were associated with classy inter-city trains, but in a few isolated cases they were relegated to commuter duties. Here at Boston South Station on Oct. 5, 1977, Delaware & Hudson PA 18 departs with a Boston & Maine Framingham (Mass.) local while PA 17 waits in the distance to back into the station. The locomotives, which D&H acquired in the late 1960s from Santa Fe for service on the New York-Montreal *Laurentian* and *Montreal Limited*, were on lease to Massachusetts Bay Transportation Authority. **(Left)** At the same location five years earlier, a Penn Central ex-Pennsylvania E8 leads ex-New Haven coaches on a local to Providence, R.I.

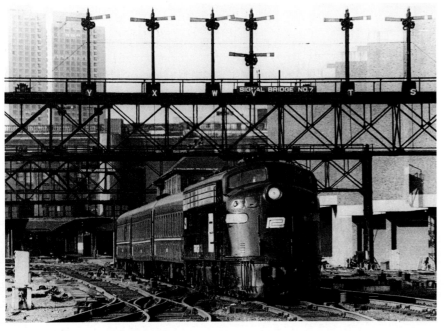

Mike Schafer

(Above) A one-car Milwaukee Road commuter train clatters through Western Avenue interlocking at tower A-2 early in the 1970s shortly after departing Chicago Union Station. At A-2, Milwaukee's main swings across C&NW's Chicago-Geneva route. (Right) Two miles in from Western Avenue, at North Western Station, Fs 406 and 407 are about to depart with trains to Waukegan (North Line) and Crystal Lake (Northwest Line) in March 1976. (Below) One of Chicago's more obscure commuter operations was Wabash's single entry, an Orland Park (Ill.)-Dearborn Station run nicknamed the ''Orland Park Cannonball.'' Wabash steam-generator GP9 495 approaches 47th Street station with the heavyweight local early in the 1960s. The service survives today under Metra (Metropolitan Rail) in the form of *two* Orland Park-Union Station trains with Metra F40s and bilevels.

Brian Cudahy

Andy Koval

4/Special Moves

John Uckley

Winding its way through the fertile farmlands of northwestern Ohio, Toledo, Lake Erie & Western 0-6-0 No. 202 (built in 1920 for the Detroit Edison Company) totes its tourist tonnage from Grand Rapids to Waterville on Sunday afternoon, May 27, 1979.

One of the more exciting developments in recent years has been the proliferation of private cars and special moves, on Amtrak and on freight railroads, and the steady increase in tourist railways. Despite the decline of the rail industry in general and the slow, hampered growth of the passenger network, it is today possible to obtain that "rare mileage" on a pretty regular basis and, quite possibly, in a luxury conveyance without equal since railroading's heyday in the first three decades of this century.

Consider, for example, the popular New York, New Haven & Hartford. The New Haven disappeared into the ill-fated Penn Central in 1969 and the Penn Central spent the next seven years dissolving. Yet today, in addition to the upgraded Boston-New York Shore Line operated by Amtrak and other lines operated for intercity or commuter service by Amtrak or Metro-North, tourist railways can take you to and through Cape Cod

(Cape Cod & Hyannis Railroad) and along the Connecticut River (Valley Railroad). The Providence & Worcester operates excursion trains on many of the NH's secondary main lines and the growing number of private cars, or private vehicles (PV's), may traverse much of this territory through arrangement with the rail carriers.

In other parts of the country, the specialty revivals are also proliferating. It seems that even if railroading is no longer in the nation's mainstream, it is still in the hearts of many. People flock to a dinner train in Iowa. Soon, tourist rail operations will serve the wine country of southwestern Michigan and California's Napa Valley. As the major railroads shed line segments and entire regions, the trend toward tourist lines and excursions will expand. Some rail lines continue solely for the seasonal passenger trade, while others maintain a more conventional freight and passenger operation.

Not too many years ago, the only way to ride the

Darrell T. Arndt

(**Above**) Private car *Caritas* dwarfs the Salt Lake, Garfield & Western centercab locomotive which pulls it during a Rocky Mountain Railroad Club excursion over the SLG&W on Oct. 18, 1986. The Art Deco-themed car began life as a stainless-steel sheathed Frisco sleeper in 1948. (**Below**) Prior to the 1975-76 journey of the steam-powered *American Freedom Train*, the 1974 *Preamble Express* train visited potential participant cities for the impending *Freedom Train* operation, such as at Boston (North Station) in this scene. The GE locomotive served for part of the train's wanderings and was later supplanted by a Union Pacific E unit painted in another *Preamble Express* scheme.

Brian Cudahy

rails in luxury was to get invited on a railroad's business car. And even the business car was in decline, as many rail executives extended their distaste for the passenger business to the company varnish. As cars of all types became available, individuals, some with massive personal resources, others with relatively modest means, took an interest in purchasing, restoring and operating PV's. Fortunately, even many of the railroads began to realize the value of business cars for entertaining customers and decision-makers and for inspecting the property first-hand and the railroad business/inspection car made a comeback. Some railroads, such as Conrail and Chicago & North Western, rostered entire trains, trailing restored E- and F-units. Others, such as Union Pacific, continued their policy of running entire domeliner trains for special company-related events and inspections, trains that made Amtrak's, and indeed many of UP's pre-Amtrak trains pale by comparison.

Through all this remains the ubiquitous fan trip, an excursion—often steam-powered (but increasingly being fielded by restored historic diesels)—operated for the enthusiast as well as the casual aficionados of rail travel. These ramblings are usually operated by rail-oriented clubs such as chapters of the National Railway Historical Society. The trains may wander diverse routings of major railroads—and the more obscure the routing, the better. Fantrip excursions have been a popular item since the first official one was operated in 1934, over the Boston & Maine and Hoosac Tunnel & Wilmington. And they remain so.

But the most exciting phenomenon has to be the revival of the PV's owned for the most part by individuals and mid-size companies. They are seen often and everywhere, and the annual convention (in 1986 at Milwaukee; in 1987 in Pittsburgh) is fast becoming quite an event for the owners, the media and PV-watchers.

The 37-mile Battenkill Railroad in Upstate New York offered excursion service using this ex-Vermont Railway RS3 and two former Lackawanna coaches built for the *Phoebe Snow*. BKRR tourist trains began operating out of Greenwich, N.Y., in 1984.

Maryland & Delaware Alco RS1 22 and two M&D wood cars make for a splendid little excursion train on April 19, 1980. The special was sponsored by the Wilmington Chapter-NRHS and operated over the former Pennsylvania Cambridge (Md.) branch. At the time, the locomotive—a former Atlanta & St. Andrews Bay unit built in 1943—was the oldest active RS1 in the U.S.

(Right) Southern Railway is often associated with steam excursions, however the railroad also knew the value of classic diesels as well. Witness apple-green FP7 pair 6141 and 6147 rolling a 12-car fantrip across Lake Pontchartrain on Nov. 21, 1982, with a New Orleans-Hattiesburg (Miss.) round trip.

Chicago & North Western played host for the August 1986 Officers of Transportation General Committee Meeting of the Association of American Railroads (AAR), assembling an impressive all-C&NW domeliner to run between California and Chicago. Union Pacific and Rio Grande co-operated in operating the special. The Chicago-Oakland deadhead move is in the Feather River Canyon near Pulga, Calif., on Aug. 3.

(Facing page) Top contender for restored classic diesels in the Midwest in the 1980s had to be Glenn and Rose Monhart's former Atlantic Coast Line E3, built for *Champion* service in 1939. Restoration was completed in spring 1983 and the slant-nose locomotive made its "re-inaugural" run on a series of excursions between Monroe and Belleville on Central Wisconsin Railroad's ex-Illinois Central Madison (Wis.) branch that summer. Here, the "Purple People Puller" glides southbound into Monticello, Wis., during its first day of revenue service.

Union Pacific operates a multitude of special trains, from steam fantrips to shippers specials to employee outings. Equipment is almost always a string of the road's handsome lightweight cars. This UP-Missouri Pacific marketing special is cruising along the Columbia River near Memaloose, Ore., on Oct. 21, 1984.

Brian Jennison

Scott E. O'Dell

Class J No. 611 of the Norfolk & Western struts across the James River between Lynchburg and Monroe, Va., on the Southern Railway in September 1982. The stream-styled 4-8-4 has trekked to all corners of the far-flung Norfolk Southern system since its restoration to service in 1982.

Sometimes even the mighty need assistance: Erie Lackawanna GP7s come to the aid of Nickel Plate Berkshire 759, which had stalled climbing to Clarks Summit, Pa., out of Scranton with a 1973 Hoboken (N.J.) Binghamton-(N.Y.) fantrip.

Wayne D. Hills

Ringling Brothers Barnum & Bailey's circus train toils over the Boston & Maine on May 1977—the first time since 1961 the circus train had operated on the B&M. GP18 1751 and GP7s 1577 and 1572 are with the famous wanderer at Groton, Mass., en route to an engagement at Portland, Me.

Scott Hartley

Tri-State Chapter-NRHS combined rare Alco road units with former Delaware, Lackawanna & Western, Jersey Central and Lehigh Valley trackage for an Oct. 14, 1984, excursion out of Hoboken, N.J., to Haucks, Pa. Power was three borrowed Centurys (two C430s and a C424) from short line Morristown & Erie.

UP's famous Challenger 3985 steams along the stretch of separated-main trackage near Laramie, Wyo., with a May 29, 1983, fantrip between Cheyenne and Laramie. Rumors abounded in 1987 that 3985 and its famous sister, 4-8-4 8444, would end active service that year.

Rio Grande's *Utah* awaits at Denver Union Station on Dec. 20, 1986, for its special assignment the following morning as the lounge car on a ski train to Winter Park, Colo. The special was operated by Phillip Anschutz, owner of the D&RGW, for family and invited guests.

Mike Schafer

Some would say it was the greatest special-train excursion run in recent years—the 1984 *Worlds Fair Daylight*, which steamed behind ex-Southern Pacific Daylight GS-4 No. 4449, from Portland, Ore., to New Orleans. The restored 4-8-4 pulled a matching streamlined consist, painted in reknown *Daylight* colors (some actually were former *Daylight* cars). **(Above)** The New Orleans-bound train glides along the Sacramento River south of Dunsmuir, Calif., on the second day of its trip out of Portland in May 1984. **(Right)** Punctuating the end of the train was ex-Great Northern observation-lounge-sleeper *Appekunney Mountain*, complete with a special neon drumhead.

T. O. Repp

5/Oh Canada!

Homer R. Hill

Canadian classics: Budd-built dome-sleeper-lounge-observation cars assigned to VIA's *Canadian, Ocean* and *Atlantic Limited* services. Car at right is on the *Canadian* about to depart Vancouver, B.C., for its trans-Canada trek; car at left is protection equipment. **(Above)** Eastbound (left train) and westbound *Canadians* meet at Ignace, Ont., early in the 1970s before VIA blue supplanted CP Rail red. **(Right)** Not all Canadian trains were famous domeliners, of course: Canadian National RDC trio at witch-hatted Grimsby, Ont., early in the 1970s was making the Toronto-Niagara Falls (Ont.) run.

It seems that in the past few decades, the U.S. and Canada have been on a see-saw when it comes to passenger service. When Canada was up in the exciting 1960's (CN's red, white and blue fares, *Rapidos*, Turbos and so on), the U.S. was in steep decline with many predicting the end of most or all intercity rail passenger service. Then the U.S. began a slow turnaround under Amtrak, while the services of CN and CP declined awaiting what became a VIA takeover in 1976.

VIA sparked an initial enthusiasm in its early years as Amtrak struggled to stay alive while it waited for rescue from new equipment and a generally supportive Congress. Now Amtrak is riding high, relatively speaking, with all indicators pointing toward steady improvement. It is VIA that is fighting for its life, as aging equipment wears out, and the government stalls on ordering new equipment, and debates rage over whether the country needs rail passenger service at all.

Canada, a progressive country in so many respects, will likely retain VIA or some form of rail passenger service, but the struggle may take a while to resolve. Meanwhile, the nation's passenger service presents a delightful blend of the old (Montreal Locomotive Works locomotives built under Alco license, steam heat, section sleepers and mixed trains) and the new (LRC's and F40's).

VIA is truly at a time of transition and there is no better time to look, in person, or through the pages of this Annual, at Canada's passenger rail system.

Roger P. Cook

Ken Kraemer

Both photos, Home

(Above) Outfitted with an array of appliances, Canadian National 4-6-2 5257 leads a four-car local out of Guelph, Ont., on the Toronto-Sarnia (Ont.) line in 1958. The survival of steam at a late date was generally more widespread in Canada than in the U.S. The Canadian Pacific 4-4-0 **(right)** taking on water while working a mixed (with a wood-sheathed combine, no less) between Norton and Chipman, N.B., harks of the 1930s. Date: June 9, 1959.

T. O. Repp

Mike Schafer

Ski trains are not exclusive to Denver & Rio Grande Western in the decade of the 1980s. This pair of BC Rail RDCs is preparing to leave the new Whistler (B.C.) depot on Feb. 23, 1986, as that road's Vancouver-Whistler Ski Train. The Buddliners provided an alternative to narrow highway 99 connecting Vancouver with the growing Whistler/Blackcomb ski area.

Canadian National mixed trains flourished into the VIA era (which began in 1977) and indeed, VIA itself operated some mixeds. But by the 1970s, Canadian Pacific mixeds were a rare commodity—CP's Prince Albert-Meadow Lake (Sask.) mixed was believed to be the road's last when photographed in September 1971 heading down toward Medstead to CN trackage to avoid a line blockage on the regular route to Prince Albert. Even on its regular route, the mixed had to use CN track for a segment—CP's Meadow Lake branch was isolated from the rest of the system.

Brian C. Nickle

(Left) Mini-streamliner *North-lander* of the Ontario Northland rolls away from the a-buildin' Toronto skyline. ONR purchased used *Trans-Europe Express* trainsets in 1977 to inaugurate fast day schedules between Toronto and Timmins; mechanical problems with the trainsets' power cars led to their replacement with rebuilt ONR F-units, such as the 1985 leading here. (Below) BC Rail's *Caribou Dayliner* is at its northernmost terminus, Prince George, B.C., in June 1986.

Alex Maye

Bruce Stahl

Early morning risers aboard VIA's eastbound *Canadian* are enjoying a cozy cup of coffee in the diner, but photographer Stahl chose to brave the sub-zero elements of Moosejaw, Sask., in March 1984 to record what has become a rare scene in the U.S.—a passenger train enveloped by fog from steam-heating lines.

Ron Johnson

CP's short cut to New Brunswick from Montreal runs right through the State of Maine. Nocturnal traveler of the Canadian Pacific of Maine was the Montreal-St. John *Atlantic Limited*, here greeting the morning sun at Vanceboro, Me., in April 1977. The little domeliner, also a haunt for Canada's only three E-units, was a victim of cutbacks early in the 1980s, only to be reinstated in the form of a now-popular Montreal-Halifax run under the shortened moniker of *Atlantic*.

John R. Taibi

Handsome MLW FPA 6768 and two mates are in command of Canadian National's westbound *Scotian* on the Halifax-Montreal run at Beloeil, Que., on a shining September day in 1974. The celebrated MLW-built (Montreal Locomotive Works) cab units would last more than another decade.

Homer R. Hill

Despite the popularity of Electro-Motive's E units in the U.S. market, only three were sold to a Canadian road—CP Rail's three E8As, Nos. 1800-1802. They were ordered for service on the joint CPR-Boston & Maine *Alouette* run between Montreal and Boston, and later worked various assignments usually based out of Montreal, including Montreal-Quebec City and Montreal-St. John, N.B. (via Maine). They lasted into VIA, but this scene of the 1802 at Montreal West station is much earlier: 1955.

(Facing page, top) Thanks to Canadian National's passenger-train renaissance of the mid-1960s, the life and livelihood of former Milwaukee Road Skytop Lounge sleepers were perpetuated. One of the unusual cars (designed by Milwaukee industrial designer Brooks Stevens) trails CN's *Chaleur* at Gaspe, Que., in 1971; they were originally built for Chicago-Tacoma (Wash.) service on the *Olympian Hiawatha*. (Facing page, lower) Another one-time regular assignment for the Skytop sleepers was the Jasper (Alta.)-Prince Rupert (B.C.) "Rupert Rocket," here skimming the shores of Moose Lake in Mount Robson Provincial Park, B.C., in August 1975. By this time, the Skytops had been pulled from this run, which under the VIA flag carries the name *Skeena*.

Homer R. Hill

T. O. Repp

Jim Ade

(**Facing page**) *Tempo* trains 70 (approaching) and 81 meet at Bayview Junction, Ont., southwest of Toronto in July 1980. *Tempo* service began on the Sarnia/Windsor-Toronto corridor in 1968 with new Hawker-Siddeley coaches and MLW RS18s—which train 71 has—but standard equipment such as that on train 80 often is called upon to protect *Tempo* schedules during times of equipment shortages. (**Below**) Mention *Canadian* and visions of Rocky Mountain grandeur spring to mind—never mind that most of the *Canadian* route crossed bread-belt country, as this 1985 scene of eastbound No. 2 near Portage au Prairie will attest. (**Right**) Perhaps a minor consolation to being 11 hours late was the opportunity to view British Columbia's Thompson River Canyon in daylight—an area usually traversed by the *Canadian* in darkness. Tardy No. 1 is at Spences Bridge, B.C., on June 3, 1986.

Alex Mayes

Alex Mayes

Greg Gormic

Bill Anderson

(Above) Dwarfed by the grandeur of the Canadian Rockies, CPR's most famous (and that could only be the *Canadian*) crawls along mountain walls east of Field, B.C., in 1974 on its westbound run from Montreal to Vancouver. (Left) CPR train 1 again, but in the more-modest topography of Sudbury, Ont., on a frigid evening in February 1978. The *Canadian*'s Toronto and Montreal sections join at this eastern Ontario mining city. (Right) Opposing *Canadians* slide by each other near Cochrane, Alta., in June 1976. Photographer was on eastbound No. 2.

The only significant purchase of United Aircraft TurboTrains was by Canadian National, although Amtrak eventually wound up with sets on a secondhand basis. CN had reasonable results with them, operating the speedsters on Montreal-Toronto day schedules. VIA inherited the trains, painting them in a flashy yellow/blue scheme, and kept them to the Montreal-Toronto corridor. Train 64, the *Meridian*, flashes through Newtonville, Ont., with a 9-car consist on March 23, 1982, shortly before the demise of the equipment some hoped would revolutionize the rail passenger market.

The Turbos have been replaced by a new breed of fast train, the LRC, whose unconventional profile **(right)** leads Toronto-Sarnia train 83 at Woodstock, Ont., in July 1982. **(Below)** There's a nip in the February night air as FPA 6791 waits to highball Brockville, Ont., with the combined *Exec* and *Bonaventure*. Brockville has long been the dividing point on the Toronto-Montreal route for trains to and from Ottawa; on this 1980 evening, the *Bonaventure* cars out of Montreal were added during the train's 20-minute stop.

Philip R. Hastings

The *Canadian* was the star train at Sudbury, Ont., but RDC3 9021 and RDC4 9200 constitute what was probably much more important to some people—local 417 to White River, loading for its departure on June 20, 1971. This unusual RDC combination with great head-end capacity was necessary to carry supplies to isolated residents of the wilderness separating Sudbury from White River, Ont.

Gil Hulin

Quick now ... who operates North America's northeasternmost passenger trains? Not VIA, but Quebec, North Shore & Labrador, whose 357-mile route between Schefferville, Que., and the St. Lawrence port of Sept-Iles, Que. (via a portion of mainland Newfoundland) is not connected to any other North American railroads. Nonetheless, the railroad—a newcomer by North American standards, having been completed in 1954—operates passenger service to isolated communities on the northern end of the route. One way, the trip takes 10 or more hours, but amenities include a variety of secondhand cars from other carriers, including full diner and (after this 1974 scene) domes. The southbound run here has just arrived Sept-Iles on a June evening behind an SD40-2 wearing the road's gray/yellow/orange colors.